Par Excellence

EDITED BY SARAH ARAK

Introduction

THE ORIGIN OF THE GAME OF GOLF HAS NEVER BEEN CLEARLY established. Ancient Romans were known to pass the afternoons by striking a feather-stuffed ball with club-shaped branches, and 15th century book illustrations show the Dutch playing a similar game on their frozen canals. The venerated Royal and Ancient Golf Club at Scotland's St. Andrews, the cradle of golf, was founded in 1754.

Strangely, golf was outlawed for most of its early history, due in part to its tendency to distract able-bodied men from the more pressing pursuits of archery and agriculture. Today, golf has a similarly powerful effect, compelling otherwise sane men (and women) to compulsively check weather reports and to call in sick to work when they're feeling fine. Since its inception, golf has distinguished itself by being one of the greatest things to do when you should be doing something else.

If you know the difference between bogey and par, can chose between a birdie and an eagle, and can point out a Redan hole without breaking a sweat, you are part of a centuries-old tradition that has become one of the most popular recreational and professional sports in the world. No matter where a golfer is, he's always at home on the green.

GOLF IS DECEPTIVELY SIMPLE

AND ENDLESSLY COMPLICATED.

—Arnold Palmer

GOLF IS THE HARDEST GAME IN THE WORLD.

THERE IS NO WAY YOU CAN EVER GET IT.

JUST WHEN YOU THINK YOU DO, THE GAME

JUMPS UP AND PUTS YOU IN YOUR PLACE.

—Ben Crenshaw

THEY CALLED IT GOLF BECAUSE ALL THE OTHER

FOUR-LETTER WORDS WERE TAKEN!

—Ray Floyd

THEY SAY GOLF IS LIKE LIFE, BUT DON'T BELIEVE THEM.

GOLF IS MORE COMPLICATED THAN THAT.

—Gardner Dickinson

GOLF IS A GAME WHOSE AIM IS TO HIT A VERY SMALL

BALL INTO AN EVEN SMALLER HOLE, WITH WEAPONS

SINGULARLY ILL-DESIGNED FOR THE PURPOSE.

—Winston Churchill

GOLF IS LIKE MONEY, SEX AND BEER—

EVEN WHEN IT'S BAD, IT'S GOOD.

—Jimmy Williams

N<small>O OTHER GAME COMBINES THE WONDER OF NATURE WITH</small>

THE DISCIPLINE OF SPORT IN SUCH CAREFULLY PLANNED WAYS.

A GREAT GOLF COURSE BOTH FREES AND

CHALLENGES A GOLFER'S MIND.

—Tom Watson

H AVE YOU EVER NOTICED WHAT 'GOLF'

SPELLS BACKWARDS?

—Al Boliska

GOLF SATISFIES THE SOUL AND FRUSTRATES THE INTELLECT.

IT IS AT THE SAME TIME REWARDING AND MADDENING—

AND IT IS WITHOUT A DOUBT THE GREATEST GAME

MANKIND HAS EVER INVENTED.

—Arnold Palmer

GOLF IS NOT A GAME OF GREAT SHOTS.

IT'S A GAME OF THE MOST MISSES. THE PEOPLE

WHO WIN MAKE THE SMALLEST MISTAKES.

—Gene Littler

GOLF IS A GAME NOT JUST OF MANNERS,

BUT OF MORALS.

—Art Spander

GOLF IS A PUZZLE WITHOUT AN ANSWER.

I'VE PLAYED THE GAME FOR 40 YEARS AND

I STILL HAVEN'T THE SLIGHTEST IDEA HOW TO PLAY.

— Gary Player

I'M NOT FEELING VERY WELL—

I NEED A DOCTOR IMMEDIATELY.

RING THE NEAREST GOLF COURSE.

—Groucho Marx

To PLAY WELL, YOU MUST FEEL TRANQUIL AND AT PEACE.

I HAVE NEVER BEEN TROUBLED BY NERVES IN GOLF

BECAUSE I FELT I HAD NOTHING TO LOSE

AND EVERYTHING TO GAIN.

— Harry Vardon

Taxes and golf are alike:

you drive your heart out for the green,

and then end up in the hole.

—Author Unknown

GOLF: A GAME IN WHICH YOU CLAIM THE

PRIVILEGES OF AGE AND RETAIN

THE PLAYTHINGS OF YOUTH.

—Samuel Johnson

FOR ME, THE WORST PART OF PLAYING GOLF, BY FAR,

HAS ALWAYS BEEN HITTING THE BALL.

—Dave Barry

GOLF AND SEX ARE THE ONLY THINGS YOU CAN

ENJOY WITHOUT BEING GOOD AT THEM.

—Jimmy DeMaret

GOLF: A FIVE-MILE WALK PUNCTUATED

WITH DISAPPOINTMENTS.

—Author Unknown

IF YOU ARE CAUGHT ON A GOLF COURSE DURING A STORM

AND ARE AFRAID OF LIGHTNING, HOLD UP A 1-IRON.

NOT EVEN GOD CAN HIT A 1-IRON.

— Lee Trevino

GOLF IS TYPICAL CAPITALIST LUNACY!

—George Bernard Shaw

I PLAYED GOLF...I DID NOT GET A HOLE IN ONE,

BUT I DID HIT A GUY.

THAT'S WAY MORE SATISFYING.

—Mitch Hedberg

It's good sportsmanship to not

pick up lost golf balls while

they are still rolling.

— Mark Twain

GOLF IS A DAY SPENT IN A ROUND

OF STRENUOUS IDLENESS.

— William Wordsworth

IN GOLF, AS IN LIFE, IT IS THE FOLLOW-THROUGH

THAT MAKES THE DIFFERENCE.

—Author Unknown

I REGARD GOLF AS AN EXPENSIVE WAY

OF PLAYING MARBLES.

—G. K. Chesterton

GOLF, LIKE MEASLES,

SHOULD BE CAUGHT YOUNG.

— P. G. Wodehouse

GOLF IS PLAYED BY TWENTY MILLION MATURE

AMERICAN MEN WHOSE WIVES THINK

THEY ARE OUT HAVING FUN.

—Jim Bishop

GOLF APPEALS TO THE CHILD IN US.

JUST HOW CHILDLIKE GOLF PLAYERS BECOME

IS PROVEN BY THEIR FREQUENT INABILITY

TO COUNT PAST FIVE.

—John Updike

SHOW ME A MAN WHO IS A GOOD LOSER,

AND I'LL SHOW YOU A MAN WHO IS

PLAYING GOLF WITH HIS BOSS.

—Jim Murray

GOLF IS A GAME IN WHICH YOU YELL 'FORE!',

SHOOT SIX, AND WRITE DOWN FIVE.

—Paul Harvey

GOLF IS SO POPULAR SIMPLY BECAUSE

IT IS THE BEST GAME IN THE WORLD

AT WHICH TO BE BAD.

—A. A. Milne

I GUESS THERE IS NOTHING THAT WILL GET
YOUR MIND OFF EVERYTHING LIKE GOLF. I HAVE NEVER
BEEN DEPRESSED ENOUGH TO TAKE UP THE GAME,
BUT THEY SAY YOU GET SO SORE AT YOURSELF
YOU FORGET TO HATE YOUR ENEMIES.

— Will Rogers

THE UGLIER A MAN'S LEGS ARE,

THE BETTER HE PLAYS GOLF.

IT'S ALMOST A LAW.

— H. G. Wells

How has retirement affected my golf game?

A lot more people beat me now.

—Dwight David Eisenhower

GOLF IS LIKE LIFE IN A LOT OF WAYS—

ALL THE BIGGEST WOUNDS ARE SELF-INFLICTED.

—Bill Clinton

IF YOU WATCH A GAME, IT'S FUN.

IF YOU PLAY IT, IT'S RECREATION.

IF YOU WORK AT IT, IT'S GOLF.

— Bob Hope

GOLF IS A GAME IN WHICH THE SLOWEST PEOPLE

IN THE WORLD ARE THOSE IN FRONT OF YOU,

AND THE FASTEST ARE THOSE BEHIND.

—Author Unknown

Fame is addictive.

Money is addictive.

Attention is addictive.

But golf is second to none.

— Marc Anthony

GOLF CAN BEST BE DEFINED AS AN

ENDLESS SERIES OF TRAGEDIES OBSCURED

BY THE OCCASIONAL MIRACLE.

—Author Unknown

I HAVE A TIP THAT CAN TAKE

FIVE STROKES OFF ANYONE'S GOLF GAME:

IT'S CALLED AN ERASER.

—Arnold Palmer

EVEN GOD HAS TO PRACTICE HIS PUTTING.

—Golf Saying

PHOTO CREDITS